SuperQuotes

for *Successful People*

Bassey A. Eyo
Brian J. Schoenborn

Published in St. Cloud, Minnesota, by Workplace Strategies, LLC.
P.O. Box 817, St. Joseph, Minnesota 56374
(320) 363-1121

Eyo, Bassey A., Schoenborn, Brian J.
     SuperQuotes for Successful People / by Bassey A. Eyo, Ph.D. and Brian J. Schoenborn, J.D.

Printed in the United States of America by
Range Printing Company
1022 Madison Street, Brainerd, Minnesota 56401
(800) 605-5982

ISBN 0-9666292-0-5

The publisher wishes to thank
Erica Schneckloth, Dave Coffman, and Trudy Trowbridge
for their assistance with this project, and St. Cloud State University
for providing us a place to learn, educate, and grow.

To our parents Asukwo, Atim, Jerome and Bernice. You gave from your hearts and for that we will always be grateful.

Introduction

Each day millions of ideas of consequence are born. These ideas are generated by those of us who decide to make a difference in our own lives and in the lives of other people. Ideas begin as dreams and unfortunately, they often stay dreams. Successful people find ways to turn dreams into reality. Oftentimes they use the wisdom of others to help them chart their course.

Successful people are made up of three components; talent, attitude and human spirit. Are you prepared for your journey toward "success"? Is your map accurate; your compass calibrated? Without a doubt, we all need a little help along our journey.

We plead guilty to stubborn optimism in the power of the human spirit. This book comes from the humble recognition of the power of the human spirit to transform one's human condition. This book will appeal to your heart as it appeals to your head, connecting them both. It seeks to restore the power of the eyes to see, the ears to hear, and the mouth to articulate wisdom for action. Most of all, it seeks to release the power of creativity to move beyond the bounds which constrain all of us. It will help you along your journey.

Humans are composed of what they have experienced. We have found quotations to be reservoirs of experiences from the hearts and minds of others — wisdom to dive into and absorb. This book is a compilation of quotations which have made an unrelenting impact on our lives, during the highs and lows. We hope they help make your life a little better today than it was yesterday, and help you stay on your personal course toward success.

"Colors fade, temples crumble, empires fall, but wise words endure."
-Edward Thorndike

Table of Contents

Life

"It's a funny thing about life; if you refuse to accept anything but the best, you very often get it."
W. Somerset Maugham

"Life is a struggle, but not warfare."
John Burroughs

"Be not afraid of life. Believe that life is worth living, and your belief will help create the fact."
Henry James

"What good is it to want to be the best if the methods you use bring out the worst in you?"
Unknown

"Life is not a problem to be solved, but a mystery to be lived."
Thomas Merton

"Life is an attitude. Have a good one."
Eric L. Lundgaard

"Human beings can alter their lives by altering their attitudes."
William James

"When you go in search of honey
you must expect to be stung by bees."
Kenneth Kaunda

"Bad isn't bad until you've seen better."
Brian Schoenborn

"Only the person who bears the sack knows the burden."
Mexican Proverb

"The quality of a person's life is in direct proportion
to their commitment to excellence."
Vince Lombardi

"You can't hold a man down without staying down with him."
Booker T. Washington

"When you've reached the point where you can accept death, then you are truly living."
Leo Busgalia

"Experience is a hard teacher.
She gives the test first, the lesson afterwards."
Alcoholics Anonymous

"What we desire our children to become
we must endeavor to be before them."
Unknown

"It is not how long one lives; it is how much.
The tortoise lives long, but not much.
The bee lives much, but not long."
Unknown

"If all our misfortunes were laid in one common heap,
whence everyone must take an equal portion, most people
would be content to take their own and depart."
Solon B. Cousins

"You are responsible for your life.
You can't keep blaming somebody else for your dysfunction....
Life is really about moving on."
Oprah Winfrey

"Words without actions are the assassins of idealism."
Herbert Hoover

"The past is history, the future is a mystery and now is a gift.
That's why we call it present."
Unknown

"Life is no brief candle to me.
It is a sort of splendid torch which I have got a hold of for the
moment, and I want to make it burn as brightly as possible
before handing it on to future generations."
George Bernard Shaw

"Don't be afraid of death so much as an inadequate life."
Bertolt Brecht

"A life spent in constant labor is a life wasted,
save a man be such a fool as to regard
a fulsome obituary notice as ample reward."
George Jean Nathan

The question is not whether we will die, but how we will live."
Unknown

"Great minds have always encountered
violent opposition from mediocre minds."
Albert Einstein

"Life is what happens while you are making other plans."
John Lennon

"To live is to have problems and to solve problems
is to grow intellectually."
J.P. Guilford

"It is good to have an end to journey toward;
but it is the journey that matters in the end."
Ursula K. LeGuin

"The limits of my language are the limits of my world."
Ludwig Wittgenstein

"The most important thing I learned in school
was how to communicate."
Lee Iacocca

"Kids learn more from example than from anything you say. I'm convinced they learn very early not to hear anything you say, but to watch what you do."
Jane Pauley

"Let us not be content to wait and see what will happen, but give us the determination to make the right things happen."
Peter Marshall

"The game of life is not so much in holding a good hand as playing a poor hand well."
H. T. Leslie

"The life of every man is a diary in which he means to write one story, and writes another."
James M. Barrie

"Life is easier to take than you think;
all that is necessary is to accept the impossible,
do without the indispensable and bear the intolerable."
Kathleen Norris

"Life. A spiritual pickle preserving the body from decay."
Ambrose Bierce

"High tide raises all boats."
Unknown

"Never confuse movement with action."
Ernest Hemingway

"Nothing in the world can take the place of persistence. Talent will not; nothing is more common than unsuccessful people with talent. Genius will not; unrewarded genius is almost a proverb. Education will not; the world is full of educated derelicts."
Calvin Coolidge

"They who are not busy being born are busy dying."
Bob Dylan

"The time to repair the roof is when the sun is shining."
John F. Kennedy

"The heart is enlarged and the human mind is developed only by the reciprocal influence of people upon one another."
Alexis de Tocqueville

"Do not wait for extraordinary circumstances
to do good action; try to use ordinary situations."
Jean Paul Richter

"Many ideas grow better when transplanted into
another mind than in the one where they sprung up."
Oliver Wendell Holmes, Sr.

"God bless my enemies and protect me from my friends."
Bassey Eyo

"It is impossible to go through life without trust;
that is to be imprisoned in the worst cell of all, oneself."
Graham Greene

"Sometimes we stare so long at a door that is closing that we see too late the one that is open."
Alexander Graham Bell

"If you have made mistakes, even serious ones, there is always another chance for you. What we call failure is not the falling down, but the staying down."
Mary Pickford

"Some people are so afraid they will go to hell when they die that they make it hell on Earth while they live."
Unknown

"Don't bother just to be better than your contemporaries or predecessors. Try to be better than yourself."
William Faulkner

"Admit mistakes and you will mark yourself
as an uncommon person."
John Tschohl

"Many people suffer from constipation of
thought and diarrhea of words."
Unknown

"Tact is the science of knowing how to get what you want and
don't deserve, from a bigger person, without getting hurt."
Unknown

"Live all you can; it's a mistake not to. It doesn't so much
matter what you do in particular, so long as you have your life.
If you haven't had that what have you had?"
Henry James

"Life is all about growing and learning and knowing that you have more ability within you than you ever even dreamed of."
Unknown

"Experience is not what happens to a person; it is what a person does with what happens to them."
Aldous Huxley

"People in the modern world think too much of their rights, and too little of their responsibilities."
Unknown

"True intimacy with another human being can be experienced only when you have found true peace within yourself."
Angela L. Wozniak

"As for me, all I know is that I know nothing."
Socrates

"He who knows others is learned;
He who knows himself is wise."
Lao-Tse

"One great use of words is to hide our thoughts."
Unknown

"Life is the art of drawing sufficient conclusions
from insufficient premises."
Samuel Butler

"The fellow who worries about what people think of him wouldn't worry so much if he only knew how seldom they do."
Unknown

"You may fool all the people some of the time;
you may even fool some of the people all the time;
but you can't fool all of the people all of the time."
Abraham Lincoln

"In life, the difficult periods are the best periods to gain experience and shore up determination. As a result, my mental status is much improved because of them."
The Dalai Lama

"Both happiness and misery spring from within; we are either happy or miserable not according to, but in spite of, surrounding circumstances."
Unknown

"Be patient to all that is unsolved in your heart."
Unknown

"He is a wise man who does not grieve for the things which he has not, but rejoices for those he has."
Epictetus

"Learn to listen. Opportunity sometimes knocks very softly."
Unknown

"If we could see that everything, even tragedy, is a gift in disguise, we would then find the best way to nourish the soul."
Elizabeth Kubler-Ross

"Were it offered to my choice, I should have no objection to a repetition of the same life from its beginning, only asking the advantages authors have in a second edition to correct some faults in the first."
Benjamin Franklin

"You don't stop laughing because you grow old, you grow old because you stop laughing."
Unknown

"You have to 'be' before you can 'do,' and 'do' before you can 'have.' "
Zig Ziglar

"He who tip-toes cannot stand; he who strides cannot walk."
Lao-Tzu

"He who is helping to row the boat has neither
the time nor the desire to rock it."
Unknown

"Watch your thoughts; they become your words. Watch your words; they become your actions. Watch your actions; they become your habits. Watch your habits; they become your character. Watch your character; it becomes your destiny."
Unknown

Passion/Human Spirit

"Nothing great has ever been accomplished without enthusiasm."
Ralph Waldo Emerson

"You can't light a fire with a wet match."
Barry Posner

"He who has no fire in himself cannot warm others."
Unknown

"If a man hasn't discovered something that he will die for, he isn't fit to live."
Martin Luther King, Jr.

"God gives every bird food ...
but he doesn't throw it into the nest."
Unknown

"Why you do a thing is more important than what you do."
Elizabeth Goudge

"Genius is one percent inspiration,
and ninety-nine percent perspiration."
Thomas Edison

"It's faith in something and enthusiasm for
something that makes life worth living."
Oliver Wendell Holmes, Sr.

"Positive anything is better than negative nothing."
Elbert Hubbard

"All ambitions are lawful except those which
climb upward on the miseries or credulities of humankind."
Joseph Conrad

"At the age of six I wanted to be a cook. At seven I wanted to
be Napoleon. And my ambition has been growing ever since."
Salvador Dali

"Curiosity is one of the most permanent and
certain characteristics of a vigorous mind."
Samuel Johnson

"No bird soars too high if he soars with his own wings."
William Blake

"Man is the only creature that strives to surpass himself,
and yearns for the impossible."
Eric Hoffer

"If you aren't fired with enthusiasm,
you will be FIRED with enthusiasm."
Vince Lombardi

"Initiative is doing the right thing without being told."
Victor Hugo

"What lies behind and what lies ahead of us is of little importance when compared with what lies within."
Oliver Wendell Holmes, Sr.

"Our ambition should be to rule ourselves, the true kingdom for each one of us; and true progress is to know more, and be more, and to do more."
Sir John Lubbock

"A man's action is only a picture book of his creed."
Ralph Waldo Emerson

"The more we do, the more we can do; the more busy we are, the more leisure we have."
William Hazlitt

"When you are aspiring to the highest place,
it is honorable to reach the second or even the third rank."
Marcus T. Cicero

"I can't imagine a person becoming a success who doesn't
give this game of life everything they've got."
Walter Cronkite

"It is extraordinary how extraordinary the ordinary person is."
George F. Will

"I believe talent is like electricity.
We don't understand electricity. We use it."
Maya Angelou

"Greatly begin. Though thou have time, but for a line, be that sublime. Not failure, but low aim is crime."
James Russell Lowell

"Live your life as an exclamation, not an explanation."
Unknown

"If you are lucky enough to be born into a situation in which you can make a contribution, you have a responsibility to do so."
Thomas Eugene Hutchinson

"Every calling is great when greatly pursued."
Oliver Wendell Holmes, Sr.

"Soul is our appetite, driving us to eat from the banquet of life. People filled with the hunger of soul take food from every dish before them, whether it be sweet or bitter."
Matthew Fox

"Perform every act in life as though it were your last."
Marcus Aurelius

"Thought is the blossom; language the bud; action the fruit behind it."
Ralph Waldo Emerson

"A noble man compares and estimates himself by an idea which is higher than himself; and a mean man, by one lower than himself. The one produces aspiration; the other ambition, which is the way in which a vulgar man aspires."
Henry Ward Beecher

"The human spirit is virtually indestructible, and its ability to rise from the ashes remains as long as the body draws breath."
Alice Miller

Vision

"Great minds have purposes; others have wishes."
Washington Irving

"You have to think big to be big."
Claude Bristol

"You can't get anywhere today if you are still mired down in yesterday."
Unknown

"Think less, imagine more."
Eleanor Roosevelt

"All that we are is the result of what we have thought."
Buddha

"You see things and you say "Why?", but I dream
things that never were and say "Why Not?""
George Bernard Shaw

"They can do all because they think they can."
Virgil

"Only eyes washed by tears can see clearly."
Louis Mann

"We go where our vision is."
Joseph Murphy

"Planning is not deciding what to do in the future.
It is deciding what to do now in order to have a future."
Unknown

"Imagination is more important than knowledge."
Albert Einstein

"Goals are dreams with deadlines."
Unknown

"Look to the future, because that is where you'll spend the rest of your life."
George Burns

"When you look forward to great things in the future, you have created reasons to smile in the present."
Bassey Eyo

"Hitch your wagon to a star."
Ralph Waldo Emerson

"A mighty flame followeth a tiny spark."
Dante

"All we have left is the future."
Hubert H. Humphrey

"The world makes a path for the man
who knows where he is going."
Unknown

"Destiny is not a matter of chance, but of choice;
not something to wish for, but attain."
William Jennings Bryan

"To accomplish great things we must not only act
but also dream, not only plan but also believe."
Anatole France

"The actions of people are the best interpreters of their thoughts."
John Locke

"You cannot teach a person anything.
You can only help them discover it within themselves."
Galileo

"The first condition of lasting happiness is that a life should
be full of purpose, aiming at something outside the self."
Hugh Black

"Far away there in the sunshine are my highest aspirations.
I may not reach them, but I can look up and see their beauty,
believe in them, and try to follow where they lead."
Louisa May Alcott

"Procrastination is the art of keeping up with yesterday."
Unknown

"Where there is no vision, the people perish."
Proverbs, 29:18

"The great thing in this world is not so much where we are, but in what direction we are moving."
Oliver Wendell Holmes, Sr.

"All successful people are big dreamers. They imagine what their future could be, ideal in every respect, and then they work every day toward their distant vision, that goal or purpose."
Brian Tracy

"Many of us spend half our time wishing for things we could have if we didn't spend half our time wishing."
Alexander Woolcott

"Just what you want to be, you will be in the end."
Justin Hayward

"Every exit is an entry somewhere else."
Tom Stoppard

"No person that does not see visions will ever realize any high hope or undertake any high enterprise."
Woodrow Wilson

"The farther back you can look,
the farther forward you are likely to see."
Winston Churchill

"To believe your own thought, to believe that what is true for
you in your private heart is true for all people — that is genius."
Ralph Waldo Emerson

"The future belongs to those who are ready."
Henry Ford

"I would give all the wealth of the world, and all the
deeds of all the heros, for one true vision."
Henry David Thoreau

"Risk more than others think is safe. Care more than others think is wise. Dream more than others think is practical. Expect more than others think is possible."
West Point Cadet Maxim

"Today's preparation determines tomorrow's achievement."
Unknown

"Too low they build who build beneath the stars."
Edward Young

"I always entertain great hopes."
Robert Frost

"Cherish your visions and your dreams as they are the children of your soul; the blueprints of your ultimate achievements."
Napoleon Hill

"What you can do, or dream you can, begin it; boldness has genius, power and magic in it."
Johann Wolfgang Von Goethe

"A person's mind, once stretched by a new idea, never regains its original dimensions."
Oliver Wendell Holmes, Sr.

"Do not be ashamed that you want so much, yet at the same time do not fool yourself into thinking that what you want today will be enough tomorrow."
Angela L. Wozniak

"We lift ourselves by our thought. We climb upon our vision of ourselves. If you want to enlarge your life, you must first enlarge your thought of it and of yourself. Hold the ideal of yourself as you long to be, always everywhere.
Orison Swett Marden

"The only limits to our realization of tomorrow will be our doubts of today. Let us move forward with strong and active faith."
Franklin Delano Roosevelt

"It seems to me we can never give up longing and wishing while we are thoroughly alive. There are certain things we feel to be beautiful and good, and we must hunger after them."
George Eliot

"I like to think big. I always have.
To me it's very simple:
if you're going to be thinking anyway,
you might as well think big."
Donald Trump

"An aimless life is a living death."
Ellen G. White

"Vision — It reaches beyond the thing that is, into the
conception of what can be. Imagination gives you the picture.
Vision gives you the impulse to make the picture your own."
Robert Collier

Risk/Courage

"The ultimate measure of a man is not where
he stands in moments of comfort, but where
he stands at times of challenge and controversy."
Martin Luther King, Jr.

"A ship is safe in port, but that's not what ships are built for."
Grace Hopper

"Not everything that is faced can be changed, but nothing
can be changed until it is faced."
James Baldwin

"You miss 100 percent of the shots you don't take."
Wayne Gretzky

"Courage is fear that said its prayers."
Unknown

"Periods of tranquillity are seldom prolific of creative achievement. Mankind has to be stirred up."
Alfred North Whitehead

"None of us are responsible for all the things that happen to us, but we are responsible for the way we act when they do happen."
Unknown

"It is never safe to look into the future with eyes of fear."
Edward H. Harriman

"It takes great courage to give up what works well now for something that you know will replace it in the future."
Unknown

"Living is like working out a long addition sum, and if you make a mistake in the first two totals you will never find the right answer. It means involving oneself in a complicated chain of circumstances."
Cesare Pavese

"If you always do what you've always done, you'll always get what you always got."
Unknown

"The important thing is this: to be able at any moment to sacrifice what we are for what we could become."
Charles Du Bois

"It is not fear that counts but the faith and fortitude we bring to life."
Bassey Eyo

"Smooth seas do not make skillful sailors."
African Proverb

"You will never win if you never begin."
Robert Schuller

"Heaven never helps the people who will not act."
Sophocles

"People cannot discover new oceans unless
they have the courage to lose sight of the shore."
Andre Gide

"The courage to free ourselves from our fears
is the beginning of our aliveness."
Bassey Eyo

"In the middle of every difficulty lies opportunity."
Albert Einstein

"Twenty years from now you will be more disappointed by the things that you didn't do than by the ones you did do. So throw off the bowlines. Sail away from the safe harbor. Catch the trade winds in your sails. Explore. Dream. Discover."
Mark Twain

"Be sure to place your feet in the right place, then stand firm."
Abraham Lincoln

"One person with courage makes a majority."
Andrew Jackson

"The greatest limitation you face is self-imposed."
John Tschohl

"Far better it is to dare mighty things, to win glorious triumphs, even though checkered by failure, than to rank with those poor spirits who neither enjoy much nor suffer much because they live in the grey twilight that knows neither victory nor defeat."
Theodore Roosevelt

"No man is ever whipped until he quits in his own mind."
Napoleon Hill

"Where there's a will, there's a way."
Eliza Cook

"The pessimist sees the difficulty in every opportunity; the optimist sees the opportunity in every difficulty."
Unknown

"Confidence is the feeling of power and strength you experience before you understand the problem."
Anthony Downs

"One of the things I learned the hard way was that it doesn't pay to get discouraged. Keeping busy and making optimism a way of life can restore your faith in yourself."
Lucille Ball

"If the creator had a purpose in equipping us with a neck, he surely meant us to stick it out."
Arthur Koestler

"No one is defeated until defeat is accepted as a reality."
Unknown

"Life is a tragedy for those who feel,
and a comedy for those who think."
Jean de La Bruyere

"To whom much is given, much is expected."
Unknown

"What we achieve too easily we esteem too lightly."
Thomas Paine

"Life is like playing the violin solo in public
and learning the instrument as one goes on."
Samuel Butler

"A pessimist is one who makes difficulties of his
opportunities and an optimist is one who makes
opportunities of his difficulties."
Harry S. Truman

"If you do not believe in yourself, very few other people will."
Unknown

"Teachers open the door, but you must enter by yourself."
Chinese Proverb

"No great plan is ever carried out without overcoming endless obstacles that come up to try a man's skill, courage, and faith."
Donald Douglas

"Opportunity may knock but it doesn't let itself in."
Gary Collins

"If opportunity doesn't knock, build a door."
Milton Berle

"Never judge those who try and fail,
judge only those who fail to try."
Unknown

"Leadership is the ability to get people to do
what they don't want to do and like it."
Harry S. Truman

"Do not follow where the path may lead.
Go instead where there is no path, and leave a trail."
Unknown

"No one finds life worth living; they must make it worth living."
Unknown

"Character is defined by what you are willing to do when
the spotlight has been turned off, the applause has
died down, and no one is around to give you credit."
Ann Landers

"Courage is the human virtue that counts most —
courage to act on limited knowledge and insufficient evidence.
That's all any of us have."
David Frost

"Leadership is a potent combination of strategy and character.
But if you must be without one, be without the strategy."
General H. Norman Schwartzkopf

"Do a little more each day than you think you possibly can."
Lowell Thomas

"Worrying is like rocking in a chair, you can do it all you
want but it won't get you anywhere."
Sir John Templeton

"No decision is a decision. You are simply the victim of the results instead of being the cause."
James W. Frick

"Good things come to those who wait,
better things come to those who pursue."
Unknown

"You may have to fight a battle more than once to win it."
Margaret Thatcher

"Everything comes to him who waits; but here is one that's slicker; the man who goes after what he wants,
gets it a darn sight quicker."
Unknown

"Fear no one, but respect everyone."
Unknown

"Life was meant to be lived, and curiosity must be kept alive.
One must never, for whatever reason, turn his back on life."
Hyman Rickover

"Either find a way, or make one."
Hannibal

"To live is the rarest thing in the world.
Most people exist, that is all."
Oscar Wilde

"Never be afraid to tread the path alone. Know which is your path and follow it wherever it may lead you."
Ellen Cady

"Safety is the most unsafe spiritual path you can take. Safety keeps you numb and dead. People are caught by surprise when it is time to die.
They have allowed themselves to live so little."
Stephen Levine

"That faith is of little value which can flourish only in fair weather. Faith in order to be of any value must survive the severest of trials."
Gandhi

"Faith is not complacent; faith is action. You don't have faith and wait. When you have faith you move."
Betty Eadie

"Although the world is full of suffering, it is also full of the overcoming of it."
Helen Keller

Love/Goodwill/ Friendship

"The deepest need in every human being
is the desire to be appreciated."
John Tschohl

"Lovers are fools, but nature makes them so."
Elbert Hubbard

"I find as I grow older that I love those most whom I loved first."
Thomas Jefferson

"People need loving the most when they deserve it the least."
Mary Crowley

"It is in loving, not in being loved, the heart finds its quest;
It is in giving, not in getting, our lives are blest."
Unknown

"Life is not lost by dying; life is lost minute by minute,
day by dragging day, in all the thousand small uncaring ways."
Stephen Benet

"One does not fall 'in' or 'out' of love. One grows in love."
Unknown

"Everyone loves a lover; we think they're a little crazy,
but they are nice to have around."
Leo Busgalia

"Jealousy is never a sign of love — only personal insecurity."
Murray Banks

"Love is an unusual game.
There are either two winners or none."
Unknown

"Love is the triumph of imagination over intelligence."
H.L. Menoken

"A friend is a person with whom I may be sincere.
Before him I may think aloud."
Ralph Waldo Emerson

"The only way to have a friend is to be one."
Ralph Waldo Emerson

"Your friend is the person who knows all about you,
and still [loves] you."
Elbert Hubbard

"The happiest moments my heart knows are those in which it is
pouring forth its affections to a few esteemed characters."
Thomas Jefferson

"Constant use had not worn ragged
the fabric of their friendship."
Dorothy Parker

"Who ceases to be a friend never was one."
Greek Proverb

"Keep away from people who try to belittle your aspirations.
Small people always do that, but the really great
make you feel that you, too, can become great."
Mark Twain

"A friend is one who comes to you when all others leave."
Unknown

"Anyone can become angry. That is easy. But to be angry
with the right person, to the right degree, at the right time,
for the right purpose, and in the right way — that is not easy."
Aristotle

"I hope I shall possess firmness and virtue enough to maintain, what I consider the most enviable of all titles, the character of an "honest person." Your honesty influences others to be honest."
George Washington

"The three hardest tasks in the world are ... moral acts: to return love for hate, to include the excluded, and to say, 'I was wrong.'"
Sydney J. Harris

"Make other people like themselves a little better and rest assured they'll like you very much."
Unknown

"We are shaped and fashioned by what we love."
Johann Wolfgang Von Goethe

"Always forgive your enemies; nothing annoys them so much."
Oscar Wilde

"No time is ever wasted that makes two people better friends."
Unknown

"No act of kindness, however small, is ever wasted."
Aesop's Fables

"Real friends are those who, when you've made a fool of yourself, don't feel that you have done a permanent job."
Unknown

"The winds of grace are blowing all the time.
You have only to raise your sail."
Rama Krishna

"The only safe and sure way to destroy an enemy
is to make that person your friend."
Unknown

"Go often to the house of your friend,
for weeds choke up the unused path."
Unknown

"A soul-mate is someone with whom we can share our greatest joys and deepest fears, confess our worst sins and most persistent faults, clarify our highest hopes and perhaps most unarticulated dreams."
Edward C. Sellner

"Be not forgetful to entertain strangers, for thereby some have entertained angels unaware."
Hebrews 13:2

Happiness

"Happiness is looking at all the good and bad in any given moment — both within us and around us — and then choosing to focus on the good."
Unknown

"Anyone who thinks money will make you happy doesn't have money. Happiness is more difficult to obtain than money."
David Geffen

"Laughter is the shortest distance between two people."
Victor Borge

"Cheerfulness is contagious but don't wait to catch it from others. Be a carrier!"
Unknown

"I am content with what I have, be it little or much."
John Bunyan

"The best way out is always through."
Robert Frost

"The happiest people are those who care more about others than they do about themselves."
Ted Turner

"Action may not always bring happiness; but there is no happiness without action."
Benjamin Disraeli

"The health of a people is the foundation upon which their happiness depends."
Benjamin Disraeli

"Happiness is, in the end, a simple thing .... Happiness is really caring and being able to do something about the caring."
Brian O'Connell

"To love oneself is the beginning of a lifelong romance."
Oscar Wilde

"The happiness of mankind is best promoted by the useful pursuits of peace. On these alone, a stable prosperity can be founded."
Thomas Jefferson

"Three things make us happy and content: the seeing eye, the hearing ear, the responsive heart."
Unknown

"Be such a man, and live such a life, that if every man where such as you, and every life a life like yours, this Earth would be God's paradise."
Phillips Brooks

"Somebody should tell us, right at the start of our lives, that we are dying. Then we might live life to the limit, every minute of every day. Do it! I say. Whatever you want, do it now! There are only so many tomorrows."
Michael Landon

"The happiest people are those who are too busy
to notice whether they are or not."
Unknown

"Remember; happiness doesn't depend upon who you are or
what you have; it depends solely upon what you think."
Dale Carnegie

"Happiness is not a state to arrive at,
but a manner of traveling."
Margaret Lee Runbeck

"The way I see it, if you want the rainbow,
you gotta put up with the rain."
Dolly Parton

"Of all the things you wear,
your expression is the most important."
Alcoholics Anonymous

"The longer I live the more beautiful life becomes."
Frank Lloyd Wright

"Work and live to serve others, to leave the world a little
better than you found it, and garner for yourself as much
peace of mind as you can. This is happiness."
David Sarnoff

"Life is tragic for those who have plenty to
live on and nothing to live for."
Unknown

"If we fill our hours with regrets over the failures of yesterday, and with worries over the problems of tomorrow, we have no today in which to be thankful."
Unknown

"The three grand essentials to happiness in this life are something to do, something to love, and something to hope for."
Joseph Addison

"Happiness is a perfume you cannot pour on others without getting a few drops on yourself."
Unknown

"When we cannot find contentment in ourselves it is useless to seek it elsewhere."
La Rochefoucauld

"To be without some of the things you want is an indispensable part of happiness."
Unknown

Service/Generosity

"I'm not important. It's what I'm doing that's important.
I could die tomorrow, but I want what I am doing to live on.
That's helping people."
Marsha Johnson

"Example is not the main thing in influencing others,
it is the only thing."
Albert Schweitzer

"A leader inspires others with confidence in him,
a great leader inspires them with confidence in themselves."
Unknown

"The high destiny of the individual is to serve rather than to rule."
Albert Einstein

"Well done is better than well said."
Benjamin Franklin

"Whoever acquires knowledge but does not practice it is like one who ploughs a field but does not sow it."
Calvin Coolidge

"Whoever renders service to many puts themself in line for greatness — great wealth, great return, great satisfaction, great reputation, and great joy."
Jim Rohn

"Knowledge is worth nothing until you share it."
Bassey Eyo

"In just a few hours of volunteering, your life
and the lives of others will be changed forever."
Craig Hagelgantz

"He is great who confers the most benefits."
Ralph Waldo Emerson

"There is no sensation on Earth comparable to what
comes from doing a kind deed for someone else."
F.O. Jones

"To give pleasure to a single heart by a single kind act is better than a thousand headbowings in prayer."
Saadi

"If our entire society is to be revitalized, it will depend on what we as individuals are willing to do on our own, in association with others, and how willing we are to extend ourselves beyond our own personal interests."
John D. Rockefeller III

"The proper aim of giving is to put the recipients in a state where they no longer need our gifts."
C.S. Lewis

"He who sees a need and waits to be asked for help is as unkind as if he had refused to give it."
Dante Alighieri

"Wealth, like happiness, is never attained when sought after directly. It always comes as a by-product of providing a useful service."
Henry Ford

"One thing I know: The only ones among you who will be really happy are those who will have sought, and found, how to serve."
Albert Schweitzer

"Only a life lived for others is a life worth while."
Albert Einstein

"The general who advances without coveting fame
and retreats without fearing disgrace,
whose only thought is to protect his country and do
good service for his sovereign, is the jewel of the kingdom."
Sun-Tzu

"I slept and dreamed that life was happiness. I awoke
and saw that life was service. I served and found
that in service happiness is found."
Rabindranath Tagore

"Only to a very limited degree do we strengthen values by talking about them. Values live or die in everyday action."
John W. Gardner

"It is not the duration of one's life that counts, but the donation."
Unknown

"There is no higher religion than human service. To work for the common good is the greatest creed."
Albert Schweitzer

"Unless you are contributing something beneficial
in some way to someone or something,
you are not an asset, you are a liability."
F.O. Jones

"When you get involved, you feel the sense of
hope and accomplishment that comes from
knowing you are working to make things better."
Pauline R. Kezer

"No one has learned the meaning of life until they have
surrendered their ego to the service of humankind."
W. Beran Wolfe

"There are glimpses of heaven to us in every act or thought or word that raises us above ourselves."
Arthur P. Stanley

"We make a living by what we earn, but we make a life by what we do for others."
Zachary Fisher

"Service is sacred experience."
Bassey Eyo

"The best use of life is to spend it for something that outlasts life."
Henry James

"The smallest good deed is better than the grandest intention."
Unknown

"What you do speaks so loud that I cannot hear what you say."
Ralph Waldo Emerson

"It is one of the most beautiful compensations of this
life that no man can sincerely try to help
another without also helping himself."
Ralph Waldo Emerson

"Strive to give back more than you take."
Brian Schoenborn

"When people forget themselves,
they usually do things others remember."
James Coco

"The highest reward for man's toil is not what he gets for it,
but what he becomes by it."
John Ruskin

"I know of no great person except those who have
rendered great services to the human race."
Voltaire

Success

"It is provided in the essence of things that from any fruitation of success no matter what, shall come something to make a greater struggle necessary."
Walt Whitman

"If you show me a person who will just do it, no matter how difficult the task, I'll show you a successful person."
Harvey MacKay

"There are three kinds of people in the world; those who make things happen, those who watch things happen, and those who don't know what happened."
Unknown

"There is only one success — to be able to spend your life in your own way."
Christopher Morley

"I never sought success in order to get fame and money; it's the talent and the passion that count in success."
Ingrid Bergman

"In the final analysis, it is not what you do for your children but what you have taught them to do for themselves that will make them successful human beings."
Ann Landers

"Preparedness is the key to success and victory."
Douglas MacArthur

"One's attitude, not aptitude,
is the chief determinant of success."
John Tschohl

"Procrastination is opportunity's natural assassin."
Victor Kiam

"I attribute all my success in life to the moral, intellectual,
and physical education I received from my mother."
George Washington Carver

"There is no end to the great things we can accomplish if
we don't worry about who gets the credit."
John Dewey

"A successful person is one who can lay a firm foundation with the bricks that others throw at him or her."
David Brinkley

"A vital ingredient of sustained success is occasional failure."
Unknown

"Whether you believe you can, or whether you believe you can't, you're absolutely right."
Henry Ford

"Successful people are always looking for opportunities to help others. Unsuccessful people are always asking, "What's in it for me?"
Brian Tracy

"He who embarks on the voyage of life will always wish to advance rather by the impulse of the wind than the strokes of an oar; and many fold in their passage; while they lie waiting for the gale."
Samuel Johnson

"The great man shows his greatness by the way he treats the little man."
Unknown

"Success lies in doing not what others consider to be great but what you consider to be right."
John Gray

"Do not wish to be anything but what you are,
and try to be that perfectly."
St. Frances De Sales

"Failure is the opportunity to begin again more intelligently."
Henry Ford

"The only place where success comes
before work is in the dictionary."
Vidal Sassoon

"Success occurs when opportunity meets preparation."
Unknown

"I am a great believer in luck, and I find the harder I work, the more I have of it."
Thomas Jefferson

"Success is the quality of the journey."
Jennifer James

"Obstacles are things people see when they take their eyes off their goals."
E. Joseph Cossman

"To find a career to which you are adapted by nature, and then to work hard at it, is about as near a formula for success and happiness as the world provides."
Mark Sullivan

"Early to bed, early to rise; work like hell, and advertise."
Ted Turner

"Action is the real measure of intelligence."
Napoleon Hill

"Success seems to be connected with action. Successful people keep moving. They make mistakes, but they don't quit."
Conrad Hilton

"One of the ominous facts about growth and decay is that the present success of an organization does not necessarily constitute grounds for future optimism."
John W. Gardner

"Some people entertain ideas; others put them to work."
Unknown

"Do what you can with what you have."
Brian Schoenborn

"Opportunity is missed by most people because
it is dressed in overalls and looks like work."
Thomas Edison

"The only good luck many great people ever had was being
born with the ability and determination to overcome bad luck."
Channing Pollock

"Getting ahead in a difficult profession requires avid faith in yourself. That is why some people with mediocre talent, but with great inner drive, go much farther than people with vastly superior talent."
Sophia Loren

"There is nothing less useful than to do a little better that which should not be done at all."
Unknown

"Personality can open doors,
but only character can keep them open."
Elmer G. Leterman

"Let us so live that when we come to die
even the undertaker will be sorry."
Mark Twain

"Common sense is genius dressed in working clothes."
Ralph Waldo Emerson

"Difficulties, opposition, criticism—these things
are meant to be overcome, and there is a
special joy in facing them and coming out on top."
Vijaya Lakshmi Pandit

"If, after all, people cannot always make history have meaning,
they can always act so that their own lives have one."
Albert Camus

"On life's journey faith is nourishment,
virtuous deeds are a shelter, wisdom is the light by
day and right mindfulness is the protection by night.
If a man lives a pure life, nothing can destroy him."
Buddha

"To be 70 years young is sometimes far more cheerful
and hopeful than to be 40 years old."
Oliver Wendell Holmes, Sr.

"To do for the world more than the world does for you —
that is success."
Henry Ford

"Deep down, everyone suspects that he or she
has the potential to be truly great.
Greatness is the real goal of every person's life."
Deepak Chopra

"Do not suppose opportunity will knock twice at your door."
Chamfort

"It isn't sufficient just to want — you've got to ask yourself
what you are going to do to get the things you want."
Richard Rose

"I feel the greatest reward for doing
is the opportunity to do more."
Jonas Salk

"Coming together is a beginning; keeping together is progress; working together is success."
Henry Ford

"Don't delay acting on a good idea.
Chances are someone else has just thought of it too.
Success comes to the one who acts first."
Henry W. Longfellow

"When you find a job that's ideal, take it regardless of the pay. If you've got what it takes, your salary will soon reflect your value to the company."
Unknown

"The journey is difficult, immerse. We will travel as far as we can, but we cannot in one lifetime see all that we would like to see or to learn all that we hunger to know."
Loren Eiseley

"High expectations are the key to everything."
Unknown

"A man sooner or later discovers that he is the master gardener of his soul, the director of his life."
James Allen

"Everyone is trying to accomplish something big, not realizing that life is made up of little things."
Frank Clark

"Let us develop the resources of our land, call forth its powers,
build up its institutions, promote all its great interests,
and see whether we also, in our day and generation,
may not perform something worthy to be remembered."
Daniel Webster

"The people who succeed are the efficient few.
They are the few who have the ambition and
will power to develop themselves."
Herbert Casson

"The joys of life consist in the exercise of one's energies,
continual growth, constant change, the enjoyment of
every new experience. To stop means simply to die. The
eternal mistake of humankind is to set up an attainable ideal."
Aleister Crowley

"Fame usually comes to those
who are thinking about something else."
Oliver Wendell Holmes, Sr.

"The shortest answer is doing."
English Proverb

"Well done is better than well said."
Benjamin Franklin

"The art of mastering life is the prerequisite for all
further forms of expression, whether they are paintings,
sculptures, tragedies, or musical compositions."
Paul Klee

"Thinking is easy, acting is difficult, and to put one's thoughts into action is the most difficult thing in the world."
Johann Wolfgang von Goethe

"Life is a gift, and it offers us the privilege, opportunity, and responsibility to give something back by becoming more."
Tony Robbins

"Keep on succeeding, for only successful people can help others."
Dr. Robert H. Schuller

"The few who do are the envy of the many who only watch."
James Rohn

"What is success?
To laugh often and much; To win the respect of intelligent people and the affection of children; To earn the appreciation of honest critics and endure the betrayal of false friends; To appreciate beauty; To find the best in others; To leave the world a bit better, whether by a healthy child, a garden patch or a redeemed social condition; To know even one life has breathed easier because you have lived;
This is to have succeeded."
Ralph Waldo Emerson